Battlefield
2
Boardroom

10 Proven Military Strategies to Combat the Business Mediocrity Minefield

Author: 2 x Global Entrepreneur
'Big Impact to Business' Award Winner

Jay Allen

ISBN-13: 978-1507706244

ISBN-10: 1507706243

Dedication

This book is primarily dedicated to the hundreds of thousands of Service Personnel, past and present, with whom I have the honour to say I have served alongside.

To the registered UK Charity COMBAT STRESS for the amazing work they continue to do for some many personnel after they return from operations enabling them to tackle the demons of their past.

And to my amazing soul mate Nicky, for the patience, understanding, unconditional love and support you so freely give enabling me to complete my mission.

Contents

Acknowledgements

My P.S.A. *"Butterpillar"* Mastermind Group for the feedback, editing & encouragement continually helping to push me further towards greater goals and higher achievements.

Capt. Andy Fenton for the feedback, editing and encouragement and insight into the most up to date military stories some of which related within these pages.

Amanda Dodd of Koogar Digital Marketing for the most amazing work done to create the most interactive website masterpiece.

Rachel Kingston of PT Graphics for the work you did with understanding my ramblings and turning it into my book cover.

Gemma Inchboard for the painstaking job of correcting my grammar in converting my thoughts into this book!

Mr. Dermot Murphy for the photography you so kindly donated in support of this project, and finally Mr. Raymond Aaron for the encouragement and insight to help me turn a long-term ambition quickly into the reality you hold in-front of you.

My sincerest and heartfelt thanks to you all.

Foreward

Ever had a bad day? Maybe not today, or yesterday, but have you ever gone home at night and wished you'd never opened your eyes and acknowledged that day ever existed? The type of day where even the rain is the wrong type of rain, and from the moment you acknowledge your awake, you know its going to be "One of those days!"

OK, so what about a good day, either today, or yesterday, have you ever woken up and said "Today's gonna be a good day"

We use the term good and bad to determine how we feel, but what determines good and bad? who measures one against the other; and more importantly was THAT DAY that bad, or was it only our perception of it that made it bad?

I'm Jay Allen, and I going to tell you why I wake up every day and know it's going to be a great day.

In 1992, after leaving college, I joined the Royal Army Medical Corps as a Class 4 Combat Medical Technician, and subsequently working all over the world as a Pre Hospital Advanced Medical

Trauma Technician eventually practicing as one of only 4 Nuclear, Biological & Chemical Warfare Medics for the Rapid Reaction Joint Nuclear Biological & Chemical Warfare Regiment.

However, after 12 successful years service, in Autumn 2002 I was diagnosed with Post Traumatic Stress Disorder, which saw me initially admitted to hospital and later for a lengthy period, attending a series of outpatient appointments, therapies and treatments, prior to my eventual medical discharge in September 2004. My career over, my marriage already broken, I had every excuse to simply give up.

However, since leaving the Armed Forces, I have held varied positions with growing responsibility, importance and authority working with companies such as Marks & Spencer, Morrison's, Balfour Beatty and the NHS to name but a few. I have been commissioned as a clinical consultant for the launch of a new product for a medical equipment company, set up and run 4 separate businesses, been responsible for the implementation of a national change management process affecting several thousand employees, sat on the national board for a H.S.E. accredited training forum, been appointed with the title Regional Ambassador by a national Armed Forces Charity, won two Global Awards for 'Big Impact to Business' as a keynote speaker and worked with one of the UK's most prolific Entrepreneurs running mastermind events, monthly seminars and given presentations to a thousand plus as a Business Growth Advisor at National Events.

I currently share my time between being Founder of the Ethical Coaching Company, My TrueNORTH providing ethical business success strategy coaching to business owners and continuing my work as a Keynote speaker, predominantly presenting at national and international conferences in regard to Communication and the clarity of YOUR message.

My support of the charity COMBAT STRESS shall remain on going as a life long quest to raise awareness (and funds) for the transformational work they do.

Throughout all my success since leaving the forces, I firmly attribute my former military training and experience as the single most important weapon in my arsenal, and over the ensuing pages, will share with you, advise you, challenge you, inspire you to STOP; consider your tactics, and ask if you've got what it takes to win this urban warfare we fight every day for survival?

However...If you already need to do something, so important that it can't wait, something so life changing that it's simply that – Life changing, then you are duly excused and can stop reading now, because I don't want to be the one that prevents you from changing your life, I don't want to be held responsible for you missing the boat and forever remembered as the one that got in the way! But, if you want to know what to do when you get to that life changing place, perhaps it may be worth reading a little further to learn how we can all achieve our goals by working together, becoming a cooperative of resource, minds, abilities, attitudes, as only by being a team, even if that team currently consists of one, will be able to achieve more than we individually thought ourselves possible.

Over the next pages, I will share with you the 10 strategies that I learnt from my time within the military that I have used to create a successful career and lifestyle since leaving.

Easy to follow and utilize strategies we can all use in our lives, our relationships and our businesses, which will have a dramatic effect on the way we operate. These 10 strategies are so profound that once we have learnt to embed them within our lives, we will no longer say I'm having a bad day. ...EVER.

CLEAR OBJECTIVES

The British Armed Forces are considered to be some of the most highly trained and one of the most professional fighting forces in the world. It has a proven track record, a history of performing, often against the odds and achieving the mission. Throughout history, its greatest achievements have been as a direct result of a clearly thought out and exercised strategy, applied with the absolute resolve there was no 'Plan B' no 'Second chance' it was dive in, sink or swim WE ARE GOING TO SUCCEED.

Recently we have come to use the word strategy a lot in business, marketing strategy, sales strategy, Customer experience strategy, employee retention strategy these days we are advised we need a strategy for everything. But what is strategy.

The word strategy actually derives from the Greek *Strategia* 'Office of General Command' used to determine the rule of battle commanded by the highest-ranking officer in the field, so from the very beginning this word strategy has had military connotations.

The Military theory behind the words is to: 'Utilization, in both war and peacetime operations, of all available forces, through large scale, long range planning & development to ensure security and victory'

Where as a slightly more diluted version in business could be described as 'Long term goals & objectives of the organization, & the course of action & necessary resources to carry out these goals'.

It was Churchill himself that professed 'Battles are won by slaughter and strategy'. The greater the General, the more he contributes in strategy, the less he demands in slaughter. Which is echoed more recently by Bill Gates when he stated 'When presented with a challenge, always take the offensive to it, not the defensive from it'.

I remember very vividly the words etched into the Barrack hut where I lives for the first 6 weeks of my Basic Military Training *"Breaketh the boy, to maketh the man"* I didn't understand for years the importance of this message, other than it hurt a lot, and appeared at times pointlessly cruel. However around 4 years later and proudly wearing the stripe of my first promotion, I began to realize the Army knew its plan for me, many years before I did. They knew who to invest their time, effort & funds in, because of a proven success strategy, that through a series of exercises and drills could determine the overall success of the soldier's career (outstanding external influence such as injury/fatality!) and from this knew the lifetime value of their efforts.

Who would be promotable, and how far they would likely climb on the promotional ladder, against those who would not, and the roles best suited to them for the longevity of time within the service.

We have begun to see psychometric testing used more and more most often with the 'white collar' job prospects, yet we only have to look to our Japanese colleagues, to see this type of testing used far more widely through schools & colleges and against almost all job opportunities. Whilst we may consider this very expensive and un-necessarily time consuming, you only have to see the overwhelming statistics that the mass majority of Japanese employee's who have gone through this type of pre-qualification testing, stay in the same employment for the remainder of their life, with an almost 0% sickness/absence record and incredibly high productivity rate compared to anywhere else in the world.

Another clear example of this this would be the incredible story told so eloquently by Ben Hunt-Davies, one of the 2000 Olympic Gold medal rowers in the England 8's. In 1996, England did not perform at the required level to win the final of the 2K mens 8's. After 4 years of blood, sweat and tears, the team failed to beat the world favorites Australia and were out of the Olympics. Throughout the 4 years, they had trained the same, eaten the same, had the same ethics, similar coaching as all their competition. Everything was comparable against every other team, yet they failed to find the right ingredients in the most important race of their lives to date and the only thing that was identified was throughout all of their training they had worked on the consideration "We must try and beat the Australians" The Australians were the world favorites, and we had entered each race with the mantra 'We must TRY and beat the Australians'.

Practice for the 2000 Olympics begun almost straight away, but with a new mantra "Will it make the boat go faster?" No longer was this a comparison with another outside force, it was an internal question of deliverance.
A clear objective that EVERYTHING over the next 4 years had only one objective – To make the boat go faster. Every moment for the next 4 years was spent considering will my actions right now, make

the boat go faster.

What I eat or don't eat, when I exercise and how often, holidays, birthdays, time for anything other than training was questioned with the simple clear objective, Will THIS activity RIGHT NOW make the boat go faster? If it will carry on, if it won't…….

The result?

Visit www.Battlefield2Boardroom.co.uk/Race and watch the race, but I did begin by introducing him as an Olympic Gold Medalist!

With a Clear Objective that is regularly reviewed, continuously identified and meticulously adhered to anything is possible. So what do you want in life? What do you wish to achieve today? This week? This month? This year? In life? What are your goals? Visualize them, write them down, create your dream wall and then set a time frame for completion. A goal is only a dream until it has a target and a deadline. It was Ted Nugent in his best selling book "Ted, White and Blue' who said all you need to achieve anything in life is a dream, an alarm clock and a dedicated work ethic.

We haven't got this far in life to 'get by'. No one at any stage of life should ever consciously think 'So this is it!' There's a whole world out there, a world of adventure and opportunity, and life is too short, too precious not to be willing to strive for more. More opportunities, more experiences, more of life.

I've also heard of people who sit and think long and hard before committing to paper something they refer to as a 'Bucket List!' A list of things they would like to accomplish "Before they kick the bucket!"

Things like:

- See the 7 natural wonders of the world

- Swim with Dolphins

- Meet the pope

- Climb Everest

- Be re-united with my children

Let me make it ABUNDANTLY clear, whilst I support the planning to do all of these things; Why would you ever spend any time working TOWARDS ticking anything off a list that says 'I hope to complete these before I die' that's just insane. Why would you put ANY effort into ticking any of them off, it suggests once you complete them there's nothing left!

Surely the RIGHT thing to do is have a yearly planner of the things you ARE going to achieve in the next 12 months. That way, not only is it done in a positive manner, but from everything you achieve over the next 12 months, will also open your mind to lots of other opportunities that you may not have considered prior to starting out, which you can add to your list for the next year.

Its this positive, goal orientated and annually achievable mindset that will ensure your working harder AND more effectively year on year towards achieving Goal after Goal after Goal.

Personal Goal Setting - Planning to Live Your Life Your Way

Learn how to set effective personal goals

Many people feel as if they're adrift in the world. They work hard, but they don't seem to get anywhere worthwhile.

A key reason that they feel this way is that they haven't spent enough time thinking about what they want from life, and haven't set themselves formal goals. After all, would you set out on a major journey with no real idea of your destination? Probably not!

Goal setting is a powerful process for thinking about your ideal future, and for motivating yourself to turn your vision of this future into reality.

The process of setting goals helps you choose where you want to go in life. By knowing precisely what you want to achieve, you know where you have to concentrate your efforts. You'll also quickly spot the distractions that can, so easily, lead you astray.

Why Set Goals?

Top-level athletes, successful business-people and achievers in all fields all set goals. Setting goals gives you long-term vision and short-term motivation. It focuses your acquisition of knowledge, and helps you to organize your time and your resources so that you can make the very most of your life.

By setting sharp, clearly defined goals, you can measure and take pride in the achievement of those goals, and you'll see forward progress in what might previously have seemed a long pointless grind. You will also raise your self-confidence, as you recognize your own ability and competence in achieving the goals that you've set.

Starting to Set Personal Goals

You set your goals on a number of levels:

- First you create your "big picture" of what you want to do with your life (or over, say, the next 10 years), and identify the large-scale goals that you want to achieve.

- Then, you break these down into the smaller and smaller targets that you must hit to reach your lifetime goals.

- Finally, once you have your plan, you start working on it to achieve these goals.

This is why we start the process of setting goals by looking at your lifetime goals. Then, we work down to the things that you can do in, say, the next five years, then next year, next month, next week, and today, to start moving towards them.

Step 1: Setting Lifetime Goals

The first step in setting personal goals is to consider what you want to achieve in your lifetime (or at least, by a significant and distant age in the future). Setting lifetime goals gives you the overall perspective that shapes all other aspects of your decision-making.

To give a broad, balanced coverage of all important areas in your life, try to set goals in some of the following categories (or in other categories of your own, where these are important to you):

Career – What level do you want to reach in your career, or what do you want to achieve?

Financial – How much do you want to earn, by what stage? How is this related to your career goals?

Education – Is there any knowledge you want to acquire in particular? What information and skills will you need to have in order to achieve other goals?

Family – Do you want to be a parent? If so, how are you going to be a good parent? How do you want to be seen by a partner or by members of your extended family?

Artistic – Do you want to achieve any artistic goals?

Attitude – Is any part of your mind-set holding you back? Is there any part of the way that you behave that upsets you? (If so, set a goal to improve your behaviour or find a solution to the problem.)

Physical – Are there any athletic goals that you want to achieve, or do you want good health deep into old age? What steps are you going to take to achieve this?

Pleasure – How do you want to enjoy yourself? (You should ensure that some of your life is for you!)

Public Service – Do you want to make the world a better place? If so, how?

Spend some time brainstorming these things, and then select one or more goals in each category that best reflect what you want to do. Then consider trimming again so that you have a small number of really significant goals that you can focus on.

As you do this, make sure that the goals that you have set are ones that you genuinely want to achieve, not ones that your parents, family, or employers might want. (If you have a partner, you probably want to consider what he or she wants – however, make sure that you also remain true to yourself!)

Step 2: Setting Smaller Goals

Once you have set your lifetime goals, set a five-year plan of smaller goals that you need to complete if you are to reach your lifetime plan.

Then create a one-year plan, six-month plan, and a one-month plan of progressively smaller goals that you should reach to achieve your lifetime goals. Each of these should be based on the previous plan.

Then create a daily To-Do List of things that you should do today to work towards your lifetime goals.

At an early stage, your smaller goals might be to read books and gather information on the achievement of your higher-level goals. This will help you to improve the quality and realism of your goal setting.

Finally review your plans, and make sure that they fit the way in which you want to live your life.

Staying on Course

Once you've decided on your first set of goals, keep the process going by reviewing and updating your To-Do List on a daily basis.

Periodically review the longer-term plans, and modify them to reflect your changing priorities and experience. (A good way of doing this is to schedule regular, repeating reviews using a computer-based diary.)

SMART Goals

A useful way of making goals more powerful is to use the SMART mnemonic.

While there are plenty of variants SMART usually stands for:

S – Specific (or Significant).

M – Measurable (or Meaningful).

A – Attainable (or Action-Oriented).

R – Relevant (or Rewarding).

T – Time-bound (or Track able).

For example, instead of having "to sail around the world" as a goal, it's more powerful to say "To have completed my trip around the world by 31 December 2015." Obviously, this will only be attainable if a lot of preparation has been completed beforehand!

Further Tips for Setting Your Goals

The following broad guidelines will help you to set effective, achievable goals:

State each goal as a positive statement – Express your goals positively – "Execute this technique well" is a much better goal than "Don't make this stupid mistake."

Be precise: Set precise goals, putting in dates, times and amounts so that you can measure achievement. If you do this, you'll know exactly when you have achieved the goal, and can take complete satisfaction from having achieved it.

Set priorities – When you have several goals, give each a priority. This helps you to avoid feeling overwhelmed by having too many goals, and helps to direct your attention to the most important ones.

Write goals down – This crystallizes them and gives them more force.

Keep operational goals small – Keep the low-level goals that you're working towards small and achievable. If a goal is too large, then it can seem that you are not making progress towards it. Keeping goals small and incremental gives more opportunities for reward.

Set performance goals, not outcome goals – You should take care to set goals over which you have as much control as possible. It can be quite dispiriting to fail to achieve a personal goal for reasons beyond your control!

In business, these reasons could be bad business environments or unexpected effects of government policy. In sport, they could include poor judging, bad weather, injury, or just plain bad luck.

If you base your goals on personal performance, then you can keep control over the achievement of your goals, and draw satisfaction from them.

Set realistic goals – It's important to set goals that you can achieve. All sorts of people (for example, employers, parents, media, or society) can set unrealistic goals for you. They will often do this in ignorance of your own desires and ambitions.

It's also possible to set goals that are too difficult because you might not appreciate either the obstacles in the way, or understand quite how much skill you need to develop to achieve a particular level of performance.

Achieving Goals

When you've achieved a goal, take the time to enjoy the satisfaction of having done so.

Absorb the implications of the goal achievement, and observe the progress that you've made towards other goals.

If the goal was a significant one, reward yourself appropriately. All of this helps you build the self-confidence you deserve.

With the experience of having achieved this goal, review the rest of your goal plans:

- If you achieved the goal too easily, make your next goal harder.
- If the goal took a dispiriting length of time to achieve, make the next goal a little easier.
- If you learned something that would lead you to change other goals, do so.
- If you noticed a deficit in your skills despite achieving the goal, decide whether to set goals to fix this.

It's important to remember that failing to meet goals does not matter much, just as long as you learn from the experience.

Feed lessons you have learned back into the process of setting your next goals. Remember too that your goals will change as time goes on. Adjust them regularly to reflect growth in your knowledge and experience, and if goals do not hold any attraction any longer, consider letting them go.

Example Personal Goals

For her New Year's Resolution, Susan has decided to think about what she really wants to do with her life.

Her lifetime goals are as follows:

Career – "To be managing editor of the magazine that I work for."

Artistic – "To keep working on my illustration skills. Ultimately I want to have my own show in our downtown gallery."

Physical – "To run a marathon."

Now that Susan has listed her lifetime goals, she then breaks down each one into smaller, more manageable goals.

Let's take a closer look at how she might break down her lifetime career goal – becoming managing editor of her magazine:

Five-year goal: "Become deputy editor."

One-year goal: "Volunteer for projects that the current Managing Editor is heading up."

Six-month goal: "Go back to school and finish my journalism degree."

One-month goal: "Talk to the current managing editor to determine what skills are needed to do the job."

One-week goal: "Book the meeting with the Managing Editor."

As you can see from this example, breaking big goals down into smaller, more manageable goals makes it far easier to see how the goal will get accomplished.

Goal setting is an important method of:

- Deciding what you want to achieve in your life.
- Separating what's important from what's irrelevant, or a distraction.

Motivating yourself

Building your self-confidence, based on successful achievement of goals.

Set your lifetime goals first. Then, set a five-year plan of smaller goals that you need to complete if you are to reach your lifetime plan. Keep the process going by regularly reviewing and updating your goals. And remember to take time to enjoy the satisfaction of achieving your goals when you do so.

If you don't already set goals, do so, starting now. As you make this technique part of your life, you'll find your career accelerating, and you'll wonder how you did without it!

So, How does it work?

Visit www.Battlefield2Boardroom.co.uk/objectives and download the Personal Planner, then use it to write down as many things as you can possibly think of that you would like to do. That's not time bound, that's ANYTHING, write down ANYTHING and EVERYTHING you'd like to do, have, try; ANYTHING. However, you only have 1 page, so for now limit it to only completing 1 page. (You are going to repeat this EVERY year, so it's fine for now if you run out of space)

ONLY once you have completed ROW A, can you work on ROW B – Timeframe. There should be a whole number of different things on your list right now, some far easier to achieve than others, ranging from rather easy and achievable targets at the start of the page, to more advantageous and interesting goals towards the bottom! So the next thing you need to do is: Using a HIGHLIGHTER pen, mark all those that are MUST DO in GREEN, those you'd LIKE to do in YELLOW and leave the rest un-coloured for now.

ONLY ONCE ROW A & B is complete can you start on ROW C. Spend some time establishing what each of these items, experiences, opportunities is going to cost? Not rough guess or estimate, but do the research make the enquiries and get a confirmed price.

It's only once we have a clear understanding of WHAT we want to achieve, the amount of time that will take and the cost than we can begin planning HOW we can make it happen.

A Friend of mine's daughter has recently announced she wishes to visit Boneo at the end of her college education for 6 weeks to attend a famous orang-utan sanctuary, but soon put it out of her mind when she learn the cost would be £4,000 per person. Being a student of extremely limited resources, she could not possibly contemplate how she was going to raise the money, which was so far out of her current scope. However, a few quick calculations and we determined she only needed to raise £8.89 per day EVERY day between now and the end of her college education and she would have sufficient to travel.

Within minutes she had determined if she didn't buy a packed lunch every day but took a home made sandwich, if she was more cautious with her mobile phone plan so she could reduce her pay as you go spend, and only 'went out' once every 9 days instead of once per week, she could raise £4,190 before the payment deadline and visit Boneo. All of a sudden £4,000 investment had become a home made sandwich, less pointless text chatter and one more night revising, her world completely changed because the IMPOSSIBLE suddenly became **I'm Possible**.

So don't look at this in despair and give up, after all, the very fact you're here right now and reading this text, is that your already on a journey, your already opening your mind to the possibility of something else, something more than you have already, and its this openness to change, to finding the clarity in determining what's right and not always what's popular, that will set you apart from the others, free you from the shackles of NORMAL and enable you to continue on this journey towards DIFFERENT, EXCITING, ADVENTURE.

For the last few years, I have created an Annual Dream-board. A visualization of the things I intend to achieve over the coming year.

My 'Dream Board' is split into 3 categories:

- Things for ME

- Things for / with Family & Friends

- Experiences

I also ensure there is a slightly 'EASY WIN' at the top left hand corner, for once I've returned from my Christmas & New Year slumber, as I need to 'kick my own ass' to ensure I'm back in 'achieve' mode, there is something not too far away as my first 'reward' so I can tick my first goal off the sheet COMPLETE, which gives me a huge boost towards achieving the other annual goals.

I've used this method of positive annual goal setting for the past few years now, and every year, the goals become more advantageous, yet every year; and with the clarity to know WHAT I need to do in order to achieve these, everything on my board has been ticked off – Complete.

Now for your business

We didn't either set up in business, or go to work with the idea of 'getting by'. None of us got up this morning and thought 'How little can I get away with today?' (Or at least you shouldn't have!) When we were young and first at school, when the chatter in the playground was all about "What do you want to be when you grow up?" the answer was never, "Overweight, over worked, under paid, stuck in a cramped house with noisy neighbours, with an old car, over due a holiday and relatively despondent to life" yet most people I have asked (and I've asked a fair few over the past 20 years) can related to at least one part of that statement!

The fact is, the majority, the VAST majority of businesses are just about – getting by, and we keep doing what we are already doing, because we either don't know what else to do, or we do; but the very thought of stopping doing something we have done for so long now to try something...NEW scares us so much that we bury our head and say things like "It could have been a lot worse"

Yet there are businesses out there that are doing VERY WELL. Growing year on year, with new offices, and new cars and share options and further expansion plans; and the truth is – It's because they have a plan! A recent study determined that almost 97% of the world's wealth is currently owned by 3% of the population, and either directly or indirectly the rest of us both work and buy from them!

So in a minute, AND ONLY ONCE YOU HAVE COMPLETED YOUR PERSONAL PLANNER I'm going to invite you to create an annual business plan. But this isn't the type of plan you submit to the bank when you want a loan, this plan is going to give you the clarity and help build a growth plan like you have never seen in your business before. This plan is simple, straightforward, requires little prior knowledge or financial wizardry, but will deliver the clarity you need to make a huge difference to you and your business over the next 12 months

Return to: www.Battlefield2Boardroom.co.uk/objectives and download the Business planner, and complete **THE GAP** exercise.

Now you have your **GAP** figure, we can start working on the many different ways you can do something to bridge it and start crossing those things off your personal planner list.

However, I must now warn you; you remember the old saying:

"If you always do, what you've always done, then you'll always have what you've already got!"

Well sadly, it is true! And if you want something different than you already have for your future, you're going to have to DO something different in order to achieve it!

So as long as you're ready to embark on a journey of change, then read on!

Oh, and don't just think that this is a 'one off' exercise. For everyone one of those goals you tick off your list completed, add two more. Life is one big adventure...go discover.

BALANCED ROLES

A 'section or squad' in the Army consists of a 'team' of 8 soldiers, managed or ran by a Corporal, with a lance corporal as the Second in Command (2IC). This section can be split, with a 'leader' taking charge of each of the halves, but with clear and designated roles and responsibilities within it. The 6 remaining private soldiers will all be gunners, with a Light Machine Gunner in each half section, a radio operator assigned to the corporal's section, and the section medic assigned to the 2ic.

In business, it's just as important to have both a hierarchy of leadership and a balance of skills across the many areas of business. In order to be successful in battle, every solider must know the mission, the goal; and if the team dynamics change

(Death, injury etc.) must be able to quickly adopt either individually or collectively the skills shortage created by this change.

Therefore EVERYONE in the team are basic radio operators, it just happens Billy was a lot better at it than the rest of us, likewise EVERYONE has done a Battlefield First Aid course, it just happened I excelled in this area, so became team medic.

The fact is, despite what everyone would have you believe, there are many businesses that 'get by' there are another significant number that 'do ok' but there are an distinct few that 'really do well' or 'truly make it' in their industry. Likewise, there are many in the service who get through, but there are a few that do exceptionally well, and it doesn't matter whether your looking at a small elite team or a brigade, from an SME through to a multi national conglomerate, there are some that appear to do disproportionately better than anyone else in their industry. It was in Jim Collins book 'Good to great' that clearly identified a key factor to this isn't just having 'the right people on the bus' but also 'helping the wrong people off the bus' and 'ensuring those who remained on the bus were all sat in the right seats' Its not just about having the right team, its about the right team having the right roles to truly flourish.

Michael Jordan the world famous basketball ace claimed 'only when an individual out grows individual ambition that team excellence shall become achievable'. But this is so much more difficult (if not impossible to achieve) if every member, EVERY member of the team doesn't fully understand the mission, and hasn't fully bought into its success at whatever cost personal or otherwise.

It takes the RIGHT people coming together to realize what they are a part of, what they are to become party to and the true extent of what that could mean NOT for them but for the wider community, the business success, that a clarity of purpose, a calling to be the very best you can be even starts to be possible. It's ALL about the people, the **right** team.

We shall elude to communication shortly, but in my experience, there is a distinct error, problem, downfall in many businesses I have seen since leaving the forces, where individuals either do not know or have no understanding or interest in the overall mission statement. It is crucial that ALL employees understand the mission, the goal, the strategy. They also need to understand their role in making that goal a reality, the part they play, and that of their colleagues, team, department etc. How many people could do their colleagues job if they went back tomorrow to find them not at work? Who could swop jobs with someone from a different team and manage to get by?

Do you even know what those who work in a different office, department, floor or buildings even do?

Sustainability isn't just about ensuring we could manage against fire or flood; it's about an in-depth and honest review of every aspect of our business and of our lives to understand where the weakest link is, and to resolve this with options. You are only ever as good as the weakest link!

Who are your suppliers? Who is an alternative replacement for when/if they are no longer an option? Can everyone have a basic understanding of what each other does? Is there a process for everything that someone else could pick up and follow? Be that who collects the kids from school and which route home do you take to miss the traffic, to who chases the late invoice, who has the burglar alarm re-set codes, and who unlocks the door tomorrow when the usual key holder is admitted to hospital, wins the lottery or is in some other means NOT AVAILABLE.

Sustainability is resilience, and that determines a clear objective, a plan, some thought and a 'test and measure' opportunity to ensure the final product is road worthy of the distance you intend to travel.

Previously within my military career I was stationed to work on an RAF flying station in a joint forces role. It's the first time I had been stationed to work with the RAF, and as such took a lot more considered approach to signing the "Standard Operating Procedures' issued to me on arrival. My rank determined I had certain responsibilities and I wanted to ensure I was 100% familiar with these on an RAF station as they may differ significantly from those on an Army Base.

I read with interest that it was entirely possible that an aircraft may not be able to stop when landing on the runway, and the emergency action drills determined it would land on an alternative EMERGENCY runway, inline with, but over the brow of a hill from the designated landing strip.

It would simply hit the throttle and 'blip' over the small mound and then have a second attempt on a longer emergency strip further on. However, I was also aware that this had never happened, and as a result service personnel had become extremely complacent and regularly used this emergency strip as an un-designated car park when they were exercising in the local woodland.
Not wanting to appear foolish, and being hastened to sign the document, I signed with the agreement that I would be allowed to immediately exercise the troops within my command to determine 'Operation effectiveness'.

The Commandant of the Station reluctantly agreed to this, and I left his office, only to immediately radio through that an aircraft was coming in to land imminently with faulty landing gear, and so would aim to land on the emergency landing strip within the next 2-3 minutes. It would give me just enough time to climb the mound to what I expected to see would be a frantic panic as over

200 drivers scrambled to remove their illegally parked vehicles from said strip. I waited and waited but nothing happened. I was JUST about to leave in the realization that my troop would need extensive training, when from no-where, the back gates of the station burst open with not 1,2 or even 3 but 7 civilian emergency service vehicles. Fire predominantly, but a police command unit and a couple of ambulances. I could hear quickly approaching various other sirens as they all begun to converge on the edge of the field desperately seeking the wreckage of said flight!

It transpired that my predecessor had also seen this rule within the SOP but had not wanted to 'make a scene' had been unable to ascertain exactly how to best manage this if it ever were to occur, so had established an un-written local agreement, that if ever this were to happen, they would simply call 999 and let the civilian authorities sort it out!

In order to ensure we are all working collectively as ONE team and not just a group of people working together its best to understand more about the roles within teams and how a better understanding of this can dramatically affect overall team performance.

How Understanding Team Roles Can Improve Team Performance

When a team is performing at its best, you'll usually find that each team member has clear responsibilities. Just as importantly, you'll see that every role needed to achieve the team's goal is being performed fully and well.

But often, despite clear roles and responsibilities, a team will fall short of its full potential.

How often does this happen in the teams you work with? Perhaps some team members don't complete what you expect them to do. Perhaps others are not quite flexible enough, so things "fall between the cracks." Maybe someone who is valued for their expert input fails to see the wider picture, and so misses out tasks or steps that others would expect. Or perhaps one team member becomes frustrated because he or she disagrees with the approach of another team member.

Dr Meredith Belbin studied teamwork for many years, and famously observed that people in teams tend to assume different "team roles." He defined a team role as "a tendency to behave, contribute and interrelate with others in a particular way" and named nine such team roles that underlie team success.

Creating More Balanced Teams

Belbin suggests that, by understanding your role within a particular team, you can develop your strengths and manage your weaknesses as a team member, and so improve how you contribute to the team.

Team leaders and team development practitioners often use the Belbin model to help create more balanced teams.

Teams can become unbalanced if all team members have similar styles of behaviour or team roles. If team members have similar weakness, the team as a whole may tend to have that weakness. If team members have similar teamwork strengths, they may tend to compete (rather than co-operate) for the team tasks and responsibilities that best suit their natural styles.

Knowing this, you can use the model with your team to help ensure that necessary team roles are covered, and that potential behavioural tensions or weaknesses among the team member are addressed.

Whilst Belbin suggests that people tend to adopt a particular team-role, bear in mind that your behaviour and interpersonal style within a team is to some extent dependent on the situation: it relates not only to your own natural working style, but also to your interrelationships with others, and the work being done.

Be careful: you, and the people you work with, may behave and interact quite differently in different teams or when the membership or work of the team changes.

Also, be aware that there are other approaches in use, some of which complement this model, some of which conflict with it. By all means use this approach as a guide, however do not put too much reliance on it, and temper any conclusions with common sense.

*To find out more about the 9 team roles, other of Belbins research or to profile your team, visit **www.belbin.com**.*

Just knowing about the Belbin Team Roles model can bring more harmony to your team, as team members learn that there are different approaches that are important in different circumstances and that no one approach is best all of the time.

So who is on your team? Are they right for the journey ahead? Have they got what it takes to put personal successes to one side in order for the whole team to survive? And if so, what role or position should they be playing within THIS team? Some of those with you now, may not be the ones that are going to see the distance, and that's ok. But you do need absolute clarity with regard to your destination, and to clearly identify who you need on your team NOW when you start that journey.

The old proverb "A journey of a thousand miles, starts with a single step" has never been more true, but stepping out together gives you far more confidence and resolute that your doing the right thing and that you have got what it takes to achieve your ultimate goals.

Understanding the stages of Team Formation

Forming, Storming, Norming, and Performing

You can't expect a new team to perform well when it first comes together.

Forming a team takes time, and members often go through recognizable stages as they change from being collections of strangers to united groups with common goals. Tuckman's Forming, Storming, Norming, and Performing model describes these stages. When you understand it, you can help your new team become effective more quickly.

About the Model

Psychologist Bruce Tuckman first came up with the memorable phrase "forming, storming, norming, and performing" in his 1965 article, "Developmental Sequence in Small Groups." He used it to describe the path that most teams follow on their way to high performance. Later, he added a fifth stage, "adjourning" (which is sometimes known as "mourning").

Forming

In this stage, most team members are positive and polite. Some are anxious, as they haven't fully understood what work the team will do. Others are simply excited about the task ahead.

As leader, you play a dominant role at this stage, because team members' roles and responsibilities aren't clear.

This stage can last for some time, as people start to work together, and as they make an effort to get to know their new colleagues.

Storming

Next, the team moves into the storming phase, where people start to push against the boundaries established in the forming stage. This is the stage where many teams fail.

Storming often starts where there is a conflict between team members' natural working styles. People may work in different ways for all sorts of reasons, but if differing working styles cause unforeseen problems, they may become frustrated.

Storming can also happen in other situations. For example, team members may challenge your authority, or jockey for position as their roles are clarified. Or, if you haven't defined clearly how the team will work, people may feel overwhelmed by their workload, or they could be uncomfortable with the approach you're using.

Some may question the worth of the team's goal, and they may resist taking on tasks.

Team members who stick with the task at hand may experience stress, particularly as they don't have the support of established processes, or strong relationships with their colleagues.

Norming

Gradually, the team moves into the norming stage. This is when people start to resolve their differences, appreciate colleagues' strengths, and respect your authority as a leader.

Now that your team members know one-another better, they may socialize together, and they are able to ask each other for help and provide constructive feedback. People develop a stronger commitment to the team goal, and you start to see good progress towards it. There is often a prolonged overlap between storming and norming, because, as new tasks come up, the team may lapse back into behaviour from the storming stage.

Performing

The team reaches the performing stage when hard work leads, without friction, to the achievement of the team's goal. The structures and processes that you have set up support this well. As leader, you can delegate much of your work, and you can concentrate on developing team members.

It feels easy to be part of the team at this stage, and people who join or leave won't disrupt performance.

Adjourning

Many teams will reach this stage eventually. For example, project teams exist for only a fixed period, and even permanent teams may be disbanded through organizational restructuring.

Team members who like routine, or who have developed close working relationships with other team members, may find this stage difficult, particularly if their future now looks uncertain.

Using the Tool

As a team leader, your aim is to help your people perform well, as quickly as possible. To do this, you'll need to change your approach at each stage.

Understanding these steps will ensure that you're doing the right thing at the right time:

Identify the stage of team development that your team is at from the descriptions above.

So take some time out and determine exactly where YOU are heading? Establish HOW you are going to get there? And then start to consider who is going to be the ones most likely to help you get there!

Are the people with you right now the right people to help you achieve your goals? Or is it likely that some of the people you are with, may have helped you get to where you are right now, but are not going to be the right ones to help you achieve all of YOUR goals? Have they already reached 'their' destination and anything further is likely to steer you off course or hinder your future?

Now re-visit YOUR destination, YOUR Journey, and really start to identify who you still need, what skills, experiences, knowledge you require in order to help you with your journey? Life is a journey on which we are all traveling, but we all have our own path and our own destination, its good to travel the majority of this with like minded, supportive and friendly people, family, friends, colleagues, but ultimately this is YOUR journey, and you have to ensure your in control of both the destination and the speed and manner in which you get there.

EFFECTIVE PROCESSES

In order to know what works and what doesn't we need to measure the effectiveness of every action, and in order to ensure we don't repeat already tried but unsuccessful actions we need to record.

In 1878, Thomas Eddison was first attributed as having designed the first filament electric light bulb, after almost 1,000 failed attempts. However, Eddison always remarked that NON of his prior attempts had failed, but were measured & recorded attempts at getting it right. Once he got it 'right' over 50,000 were produced within the next 12 months. Was Eddison a scientist or entrepreneur? Well, he may have a science background, but he went on to found 14 Companies including G.E. (General Electric), which continues to be one of the largest publically, traded companies in the world.

As already mentioned, the British Armed Forces are revered as some of the most highly training, professional fighting force in the world. Why, because we have a well-tried and tested system of ensuring we get it right. I remember my first every Regimental Sergeant Major WO1 Best, advising me *"Allen, if there is ever a need to move many people, or many things anywhere in the world, never worry or fear, as we are the best in the world of getting many people and many things to the right place at the right time. If however, you have a personal problem, and need something just for you; do it in your own time; as were too busy moving many people and many things"* This proved to be invaluable advise; whenever Regiments, Battalions moved from one country to another, not a single item went missing; whereas, as a Medic working within a Corps (rather than a regiment) you were often posted individually and I have heard many a story about soldiers turning up for work at their new unit, only to find them in a different country, or their belongs being shipped to Afghanistan, or the Falkland's.

In business it's vital to 'test and measure'. Look at your systems, try them, test them, see if they are robust, find the cracks, determine their effectiveness; then once it's all over and you've made the necessary adjustments, start again.

I previously had the opportunity to work with one of the BBC Radio DJ's during his phone in sessions. I would attend their reception desk, get signed in, meet with the producer who would guide me through the maize of corridors to the studio, where I would sit and wait for a suitable point to enter and get ready for the phone in session. On one particular session, I arrived to what appear to be chaos; everyone was rushing around somewhat disorganized in a frenzy of uncertainty.

The producer offered apologies, pointed me towards a coffee machine and said 'we'll get to you in a bit' before dashing back off to the hype of excitement. I later learnt that the show had almost not gone out at all that day! It would appear, the researcher for the program was a guy called Sam, whom everyone emailed their requirements, and Sam diligently did the necessary research and emailed them his findings. However, Sam was on leave! Organized, pre-booked, approved time off! But Sam's leave had not been communicated throughout the team nor had Sam implemented an Auto-responder to advise people of his lack of attendance) The whole system had come to a crashing halt because of an unwritten, expected reliance on Sam!

Any business is bigger than an individual, ANY individual. A successful business has sufficient systems and process to enable ANYONE not to turn up tomorrow morning and the process can be followed and the wheels keep turning.

This has never been so evident as the military and the 'keen, green, fighting machine' it's bums on seats working as one for a collective goal. But, any one bum is missing and the mission continues, someone simply designates roles & responsibilities and the show goes on.

It may appear a little drastic, but the only way you have both sustainability and scalability is by recording your actions, good and bad to determine what works, and what doesn't. What and WHO is effective and not! We need people ON THE BUS; we don't want people coming along for a free ride!

So I want you to spend tomorrow recording EVERYTHING. There should be a 'Standard Operating Procedures' in EVERY business, that's regularly tested, checked, updated and amended. Test and measure EVERYTHING in your business, you need to know that if EVERYONE didn't come in tomorrow, a brand new team could follow a series of instructions and the wheels of commerce would keep turning.

Now you have your Standard Operating Procedure (SOP), you've tested it and you're happy it works, begin the next phase of testing! – **'What if?'**

What if, is the next level of processes, for when the first process breaks! MI5 & MI6 aren't incidental; they play a pivotal role in surveillance, counter terrorism, strategic and contingency planning. For EVERY part of your current plan, you need at least a Plan B! a What if? The devils advocate of all plans that pulls to pieces everything you've just worked so hard to put right, to see if you can built it again, bigger, better, faster, smarter they scrutinize EVERY last detail asking what if? What if? What if? Until your back at the beginning. There are people stuck in darkened rooms within Whitehall whose full time, permanent role is to ask What if? And then write and test the theory to determine likelihood and overall outcome.

I've been on too many an exercise in the middle of the night, traipsing round the back end of now-where whilst the contingency plan is being measured to know this happens all the time, and its because it happens so frequently that when (not if) the unforeseen occurs, instead of panic and confusion, its simply 'switch to plan B' and carry on. It's this type of endless scrutiny of every facet of your business that will teach you the flaws; the weaknesses you need to consider ensuring you have everything covered off and capable to succeed.

Benefits of processes, procedures and standards

Developing processes, procedures and standards is particularly important if you are in the early stages of establishing a business, or when you are trying to rebuild or grow a business that has been underperforming.

Business processes, procedures and standards are vital for training staff and induction programs, as well as formal processes like staff performance reviews.

Processes and procedures

Having formalized processes and procedures for your business can save you time and money by increasing efficiency. Staff can get more done in less time by following set processes and procedures, and you can spend less time overseeing the day-to-day running of the business.

Processes and procedures can also improve the consistency of product and service delivery by your staff.

Standards and policies

By creating standards and policies for your business, you set benchmarks that your staff must meet.

For example, you may have a standard for serving customers that involves being courteous, completing transactions within a certain time, and doing everything in your power to accommodate customer requests. This can improve the experience of your customers, suppliers and/or distributors in their dealings with you.

Customers who have a positive experience are more likely to become repeat customers, and are less likely to complain about your business.

Standardising key business activities

It's important to create processes, procedures and standards for your key business activities. Depending on your individual business, these may include:

- Customer service (including a customer service program)
- Sales practices and sales policies (e.g. guarantees, warranties and refunds)
- Marketing and promotion (including online marketing and social media)
- Staff training and performance reviews
- Energy efficiency and environmental considerations (e.g. water restrictions)
- Management responsibilities

- Record keeping, reporting and money management
- Use of technology (e.g. rules around staff internet usage).
- How to create effective processes, procedures and standards

In order for all of your business's processes, procedures and standards to be effective, they must be:

- Documented (e.g. it's a good idea to create a 'standard operating procedures' manual)
- Grounded in the vision and strategy of your business
- Clear about general business procedures as well as role-specific procedures
- Part of your staff training program, and made available in a user-friendly format afterwards (e.g. on paper or electronically as a PDF)
- Practiced by management, so other staff will follow lead
- Discussed regularly in meetings (including positive and negative feedback)
- Flexible and open to improvement
- Designed to empower and inform, rather than constrain staff
- Regularly reviewed and updated (especially due to legislative or compliance changes that affect your business).

Having said all that, there is also a counter argument that too many systems, processes and procedures stifle growth and create interdependence on bureaucracy and red tape. Having read with much interest an article we shall discuss in much more detail later in the book regarding Management & Leadership, there is a fabulous quote regarding the use of Systems & Processes:

"Management requires Systems & Process, but leadership beats management and culture eats leadership for breakfast!"

So, perhaps we ought to aim for creating the right culture, developing proactive leadership in order not to be totally reliant of Systems and process driven management!

Now, before you go any further, you got it, **What if**?....

Its time to re-check the basics to ensure those corners aren't being cut and you're still on track. It may well be a good idea to run some robust 'sustainability tests' to determine how effective your processes are.

Why not consider a 'Secret Shopper' a bogus enquiry or two to determine if things work the way they should. I certainly remember fondly the amount of time whilst we were stationed in Barracks the fun we would have trying to break into a fellow regiments barracks and if successful leave something distinctly memorable to say we had been there. Whilst from the outside may seem like a childish and dangerous prank, it was an incredible serious operation to assist others in maintain vigilance and continually testing each others processes to ensure it's a friendly feedback report we get afterwards and not a hostile takeover!

So test, measure and record the results for everything within your business. Encourage your team to also ask the 'What if?...' questions for the things you haven't even considered and consider EVERYTHING to determine your Strengths and Weaknesses, what is an Opportunity and what could ultimately become a threat to your mission success.

GOOD COMMUNICATION

There are currently over 170,000 words in the English Dictionary of which (depending on such things as sex, class, age, profession, dialect) we use around 10-14,000 every day. However as the actual words only make up less than 35% of communication with non verbal communication making up the rest it is vitally important for us to realize it's as important if not more important to be aware of both the right language both verbal and non verbal.

One of my first childhood, school memories was when I was 5-6 years old, during the dinner break at junior school, standing around outside with a group of other boys from my class hovering around the PT teacher – Mr. Strachan. Mr. Strachan asked each of us "What do you want to be when you grow up?" and the usual answers of footballer, pop star, astronaut etc.
were all heard around me. But me (being me) said "Bigger!" you see it's the entirely wrong question to ask, life should not be based around what do you want to be, but WHO do you want to be.

I don't want to be a footballer; I've seen enough drunken 50yr olds who badly kick a ball with their grandkids on a Sunday afternoon in the park who profess to be footballers to know I don't want to be one of them. I've seen too many Redtop newspapers with extensive zoom lens camera's poking their nose into some Z list has been band member, as they embarrass themselves whilst on holiday only to learn they are now on the front of the paper the next morning to know I don't want to be one of them either.

You see its not WHAT do you want to be, its WHO?

I want to be someone who others respect, value the opinion of, consider a trusted and loyal friend. Someone who is able to enjoy life and all it has to throw at them, and leaves a lasting impression on all those he meets. I don't particularly want to be famous, I don't expect to be popular, I'd just like to get through life being the best I can be.

Therefore, when it comes to language, and the most important lesson we can learn, is how to correctly, and accurately ensure the language we use, both verbally and non verbally is the most fitting for the circumstances we find ourselves in, and not only consider what our intent is, but measure and respond to how this is being received.

In the military we are duty bound to follow ORDERS. These are often short, sharp commands that are followed immediately and without question. This is developed through countless hours, days, weeks, months sometimes throughout your military career conducting Military drill. These 'drills' become ingrained, so that a solider carries out an action without conscious thought, as a subconscious reaction to the command. I've now been left the military for over 10 years, however on 11 November every year I dress in my military attire, make my way to meet with my many comrades past & present within the Royal British Legion, form up and march to the cenotaph to pay my respects for fallen colleagues. The moment the drill Sargent utters the command, hundreds of 'individuals' suddenly jump back to being a 'body of men' backs straighten, necks in the back of the collar, heels smash to the ground in unison as we stand to attention.

A drill taught for countless hours on the drill squares of our past, runs through your veins like it were yesterday and you react, immediately, responsively, without question or reservation. The clarity of that word 'SHUN' cuts through all others and brings men and women from around the world from being an individual to being part of something far bigger than you or I.

Time spent on the firing range was just as important that communication had the clarity the severity of the circumstance deserved, and so on every occasion where a 'live fire' order is being given, regardless of whatever else is happening around you, the order must be given twice! This CLARITY of communication was paramount in ensuring everybody understood with absolute clarity the WHAT, WHERFOR, and WHY of any action or reaction.

I remember fondly the expression of my grandmother 'You have 2 ears but only 1 mouth' implying if we spent twice as much time listening as we did talking, we would be far wiser but it also transpires we would need to use far less words to ensure we are understood. The science of NLP looks amongst many other things, far more closely at the verbal & non verbal communication we all use and its effectiveness; however you don't need a masters degree to understand we all communicate differently, and perhaps if we spent more time reviewing the communication of others and how to consider, amend and modify our own language to suit both our environment, the audience and the intentions of our communication, we would see far more effective responses.

There is also a great deal to be said about simplicity. In an age full of words, both of ours and others, at a time where we are often bombarded with sales, offers, 24Hr news, 100% connectivity, its easy to miss the point, blend in and get missed. In order to stand out both as an individual and within our business, we need a strong, powerful message, that's easily understood, easily shared, easy to remember and intriguing enough for people to WANT to know more.

With Google now considered THE search engine of choice across the world, and so many hundreds of thousands of opportunities and choices at our finger tips its never been more important for our voice, our mission, to be heard through the noise of everything else in life. We must therefore manage and maintain our message be encouraged to be passed on with such clarity that your asked for by name, not searched for by sector or category.

In an age where there is more information shared in open forum every year, than has ever been recorded in the doomsday book, its never been more important to ensure our message is noticed. It's often LESS is more! But clarity is king.

The Army went to exceptional lengths to protect their data. Continually updating the security algorithms and personnel to ensure not one person every had full access and that anything they did have access to was never enough to in itself cause a threat. I'm encouraging you to collect data, mass amounts of data, to start LISTENING again and not just hearing, because those little nuances of information that appear either in conversation or online, could make the difference between success and failure. But its just as vital that your able to record this information in such a manner that it doesn't then become a threat.

The cyber hackers of the world challenge themselves all the time the source, crack and share data. Your data supremacy only remains so, whilst it's not the common knowledge of all. I was subjected to espionage within my first business since leaving the forces, when a sacked employee was able to gain access to our customer database prior to leaving, only for me to find she had sold it to our competitor who then knew exactly who to approach, what to offer them and at what cost to do some serious damage to our relationships and business growth.

Today's friend can easily become tomorrows foe, so remain alert, cautious and considerate with your most valuable asset.

So what is GOOD communication?

Whenever you communicate with someone else, you and the other person follow the steps of the communication process shown below:

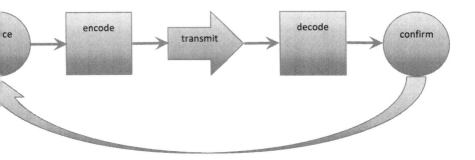

Here, the person who is the source of the communication encodes it into a message, and transmits it through a channel. The receiver decodes the message, and, in one way or another, feeds back understanding or a lack of understanding to the source.

By understanding the steps in the process, you can become more aware of your role in it, recognize what you need to do to communicate effectively, anticipate problems before they happen, and improve your overall ability to communicate effectively.

The sections below help you do this, and help you improve the way you communicate at each stage of the process.

The Source – Planning Your Message

Before you start communicating, take a moment to figure out what you want to say, and why. Don't waste your time conveying information that isn't necessary – and don't waste the listener or reader's time either. Too often, people just keep talking or keep writing – because they think that by saying more, they'll surely cover all the points. Often, however, all they do is confuse the people they're talking to.

To plan your communication:

- Understand your objective. Why are you communicating?

- Understand your audience. With whom are you communicating? What do they need to know?

- Plan what you want to say, and how you'll send the message.

- Seek feedback on how well your message was received.

When you do this, you'll be able to craft a message that will be received positively by your audience.

Good communicators use the KISS ("Keep It Simple and Straightforward") principle.

They know that less is often more, and that good communication should be efficient as well as effective.

Encoding – Creating a Clear, Well-Crafted Message

When you know what you want to say, decide exactly how you'll say it. You're responsible for sending a message that's clear and concise. To achieve this, you need to consider not only what you'll say, but also how you think the recipient will perceive it.

We often focus on the message that we want to send, and the way in which we'll send it. But if our message is delivered without considering the other person's perspective, it's likely that part of that message will be lost. To communicate more effectively:

- Understand what you truly need and want to say.

- Anticipate the other person's reaction to your message.

- Choose words and body language that allow the other person to really hear what you're saying.

With written communication, make sure that what you write will be perceived the way you intend. Words on a page generally have no emotion – they don't "smile" or "frown" at you while you're reading them (unless you're a very talented writer, of course!)

When writing, take time to do the following:

- Review your style.

- Avoid jargon or slang.

- Check your grammar and punctuation.

- Check also for tone, attitude, nuance, and other subtleties. If you think the message may be misunderstood, it probably will. Take the time to clarify it!

- Familiarize yourself with your company's writing policies.

Another important consideration is to use pictures, charts, and diagrams wherever possible. As the saying goes, "a picture speaks a thousand words."

Also, whether you speak or write your message, consider the cultural context. If there's potential for miscommunication or misunderstanding due to cultural or language barriers, address these issues in advance. Consult with people who are familiar with these, and do your research so that you're aware of problems you may face.

Choosing the Right Channel

Along with encoding the message, you need to choose the best communication channel to use to send it. You want to be efficient, and yet make the most of your communication opportunity.

Using email to send simple directions is practical. However, if you want to delegate a complex task, an email will probably just lead to more questions, so it may be best to arrange a time to speak in person. And if your communication has any negative emotional content, stay well away from email! Make sure that you communicate face to face or by phone, so that you can judge the impact of your words and adjust these appropriately.

When you determine the best way to send a message, consider the following:

- The sensitivity and emotional content of the subject.

- How easy it is to communicate detail.

- The receiver's preferences.

- Time constraints.

- The need to ask and answer questions.

Decoding – Receiving and Interpreting a Message

It can be easy to focus on speaking; we want to get our points out there, because we usually have lots to say. However, to be a great communicator, you also need to step back, let the other person talk, and just listen.

This doesn't mean that you should be passive. Listening is hard work, which is why effective listening is called active listening.

To listen actively, give your undivided attention to the speaker:

- Look at the person.

- Pay attention to his or her body language.

- Avoid distractions.

- Nod and smile to acknowledge points.

- Occasionally think back about what the person has said.

- Allow the person to speak, without thinking about what you'll say next.

- Don't interrupt.

- Empathic listening also helps you decode a message accurately.

To understand a message fully, you have to understand the emotions and underlying feelings the speaker is expressing. This is where an understanding of body language can be useful.

FEEDBACK

You need feedback, because without it, you can't be sure that people have understood your message. Sometimes feedback is verbal, and sometimes it's not. We've looked at the importance of asking questions and listening carefully. However, feedback through body language is perhaps the most important source of clues to the effectiveness of your communication.

By watching the facial expressions, gestures, and posture of the person you're communicating with, you can spot:

- Confidence levels.

- Defensiveness.

- Agreement.

- Comprehension (or lack of understanding).

- Level of interest.

- Level of engagement with the message.

- Truthfulness (or lying/dishonesty).

As a speaker, understanding your listener's body language can give you an opportunity to adjust your message and make it more understandable, appealing, or interesting. As a listener, body language can show you more about what the other person is saying. You can then ask questions to ensure that you have, indeed, understood each other. In both situations, you can better avoid miscommunication if it happens.

Feedback can also be formal. If you're communicating something really important, it can often be worth asking questions of the person you're talking to make sure that they've understood fully. And if you're receiving this sort of communication, repeat it in your own words to check your understanding.

It can take a lot of effort to communicate effectively. However, you need to be able to communicate well if you're going to make the most of the opportunities that life has to offer.

By learning the skills you need to communicate effectively, you can learn how to communicate your ideas clearly and effectively, and understand much more of the information that's conveyed to you.

As either a speaker or a listener, or as a writer or a reader, you're responsible for making sure that the message is communicated accurately.

Pay attention to words and actions, ask questions, and watch body language. These will all help you ensure that you say what you mean, and hear what is intended.

We need only look at the amount of corporate waffle, buzz words and clichés used to see how complicated it could be to cut through it all to the essence of the message; and how quickly a message can get lost by 'over dressing' it with metaphor, and on that note, I shall STOP!

LEADERSHIP, SUPPORT & TRUST

Some people were born leaders, others have to learn to become leaders, but if push came to shove I certainly believe EVERYONE can lead. There are many styles of leadership and many methods to lead, it is often useful to be able to determine a number and be able to use more than one style depending on the persons you are leading, the circumstance, the goal/mission, and the desired outcome. Some leaders are charismatic, inspirational and lead from the front, others less extrovert but have influence over those who are and able to lead from aside, others are more introverts and tend to drive through change, policy, rules, processes from the rear. In larger institutions there is a need for a combination of these leadership styles, dependent on both role, and function. However, we must also understand there is a colossal difference between Leadership and Management.

Management is to follow a process, getting everyone together to follow a process to accomplish desires goals / objectives. Leadership is based more on influence, and therefore doesn't require process to achieve outcomes.

During World War 1, Surgeon Captain Arthur Martin Leake R.A.M.C. was awards the Victoria Cross not once but twice, for approaching and attending to many injured foot soldiers whilst under close heavy fire, being shot three times, but refusing aide until all around him had been treated. Only 11 months later to do almost the same again, whilst waving a white flag; advanced to an injured soldier in heavy oncoming fire, and when his hand carrying the white flag was shot, was heard to shout "You'll have to do better than that, I've got another one" before picking up the flag in the other hand and continuing to attend to the injured soldier.

This courageous act of un-selfless bravery, was not only inspirational leadership which saw so many other medics at the time continue to attend to the injured, but has gone on to inspire so many other young men joining the Royal Army Medical Corps after one of the two Training Platoons through Soldiers Basic Training is named after him.

My last Commanding Officer, was much less a good Manager than an inspirational Leader, and although renown for being maverick by his colleagues, was so inspirational to those he managed, that when he was due to be posted, no less than 47 of his management team requested to move with him. This was by no means because he was a great manager, nor that he was so adored by all who served under him, more that he was such an inspirational leader, that anyone else simply didn't measure up to his courageous efforts to forge his own path come what may and ensure his name and efforts were duly recognized for everything he (and those who followed him) assisted him in achieving. He has subsequently gone on to become the second highest-ranking officer in his field across all three services and has maintained his highly admired maverick approach throughout.

However, a ruthless leader may very well quickly have no-one left to lead, so support and trust are also vital components to consider.

On the 26th May 2000 my sons mother and I separated. This was a very harrowing and difficult time, and sadly by no means the harmonious separation I would have wanted. We were living in Germany at the time, and I had just returned from operations overseas. Very shortly afterwards, she had packed everything, taken car, money and passport and returned to the UK. I was left with no money, no transport and no passport to follow and determine where she or my son had relocated. One evening the following week, a soldier, junior in rank to myself; and not someone I knew that well at all; appeared at my door within the mess and instructed me to "Follow me" Somewhat uncertain, any caring as to what was going on, I followed to find him present me with a old but road-worthy car (With ownership documents in my name), money, clothes and a military leave warrant signed by a senior officer. "Go and find your son" he said and then turned and left me in the night. Such an unselfish act of support by someone with whom I had little prior knowledge or recognition of, demonstrates the same fine qualities previously described by such a successful Leader as I have recently mentioned, and I can testify whole heartedly, the trust and support gained by this type of leadership goes beyond any other. I have never forgotten that moment Lance Corporal Paul Scrace, you are forever in my thanks and prayers.

In business, we need to ensure we create a culture of support and trust. Support for our fellow colleagues and trust in the leadership and management to visualize and focus on the objectives. I have already eluded to Jim Collins (Good to Great) and it was interesting to see that a characteristic of some of the most successful companies (across various sectors) that although there was significant 'debate' within the management structure regarding the current and future direction of the business, once a decision had been reached, those who were going to become the most successful saw a quick alliance of EVERYONE getting behind the plan. Despite how severe the questioning of the decisions regarding one direction or another, those who had the most impact on success were the ones where the team collectively pulled together and saw the plan through, ALL the way through to completion.

Within my own experience in the military, the quickest route to promotion and further success was quickly identify a successor for your role and aspire to become the next successor of your line manager. It was about spending 80% of your time; effort and energy being the best you could possibly be at the role your in and 25%! Of your time, effort and energy understanding the role you wished to aspire to. (And before you make comment about my math: Yes, it did take an additional magical 5% element of Blood, Sweat and Absolute determination!)

It was about being content with where you were right now and understanding the 'bigger picture' and why it was vitally important that YOU had been picked for the role you were currently in, whilst still looking to the future and where the business was heading and aspiring to be seen for what else you could offer.

I still remember well, both my English and my Drama teachers from secondary school. Not particularly for their teaching expertise or experience (although I'm sure they were both exceptional) but for the clarity of inspiration they created within each of us as pupils. We understood with more clarity than in any other subject the role we had to carry out right there and then, each lesson, each session and how it in some little way contributed to the 'big picture'. But it was done in such an inspiration way, that the 2nd assistant scene designer felt proud in the same way the leading role did. Both Kate Lake, and Mick Flowers knew exactly how to get the most out of every single person on the team without being a larger than life character themselves, but their leadership and support from either the front, side or rear, created a team ethic of trust, which went on to produce more professional actors than any other school in the county, year after year.

So how do we Bring LEADERSHIP skills together

1. Creating an Inspiring Vision of the Future

In business, a vision is a realistic, convincing and attractive depiction of where you want to be in the future. Vision provides direction, sets priorities, and provides a marker, so that you can tell that you've achieved what you wanted to achieve.

To create a vision, leaders focus on an organization's strengths by using tools such as Porter's Five Forces, PEST Analysis, USP Analysis, Core Competence Analysis and SWOT Analysis to analyse their current situation. They think about how their industry is likely to evolve, and how their competitors are likely to behave. They look at how they can innovate successfully, and shape their businesses and their strategies to succeed in future marketplaces.

They then test their visions with appropriate market research, and by assessing key risks using techniques such as Scenario Analysis.

Therefore, leadership is proactive – problem solving, looking ahead, and not being satisfied with things as they are.

Once they have developed their visions, leaders must make them compelling and convincing. A compelling vision is one that people can see, feel, understand, and embrace. Effective leaders provide a rich picture of what the future will look like when their visions have been realized. They tell inspiring stories, and explain their visions in ways that everyone can relate to.

Here, leadership combines the analytical side of vision creation with the passion of shared values, creating something really meaningful to the people being led.

2. Motivating and Inspiring People

A compelling vision provides the foundation for leadership. But it's leaders' ability to motivate and inspire people that help them deliver that vision.

For example, when you start a new project, you will probably have lots of enthusiasm for it, so it's often easy to win support for the project at the beginning. However, it can be difficult to find ways to keep your vision inspiring after the initial enthusiasm fades, especially if the team or organization needs to make significant changes in the way that they do things. Leaders recognize this, and they work hard throughout the project to connect their vision with people's individual needs, goals, and aspirations.

One of the key ways they do this is through Expectancy Theory. Effective leaders link together two different expectations:

- The expectation that hard work leads to good results.
- The expectation that good results lead to attractive rewards or incentives.

This motivates people to work hard to achieve success, because they expect to enjoy rewards – both intrinsic and extrinsic – as a result.

Other approaches include restating the vision in terms of the benefits it will bring to the team's customers, and taking frequent opportunities to communicate the vision in an attractive and engaging way.

What's particularly helpful here is where leaders have expert power. People admire and believe in these leaders because they are expert in what they do. They have credibility, and they've earned the right to ask people to listen to them and follow them. This makes it much easier for these leaders to motivate and inspire the people they lead.

Leaders can also motivate and influence people through their natural charisma and appeal, and through other sources of power, such as the power to pay bonuses or assign tasks to people. However, good leaders don't rely too much on these types of power to motivate and inspire others.

3. Managing Delivery of the Vision

This is the area of leadership that relates to management. According to the Hersey-Blanchard Situational Leadership Model, there is a time to tell, a time to sell, a time to participate, and a time to delegate. Knowing which approach you need to use, and when you need it, is key to effective leadership.

Leaders must ensure that the work needed to deliver the vision is properly managed – either by themselves, or by a dedicated manager or team of managers to whom the leader delegates this responsibility – and they need to ensure that their vision is delivered successfully.

To do this, team members need performance goals that are linked to the team's overall vision. For day-to-day management of delivering the vision, the Management By Wandering Around (MBWA) approach helps to ensure that what should happen, really happens.

Leaders also need to make sure they manage change effectively. This helps to ensure that the changes needed to deliver the vision are implemented smoothly and thoroughly, with the support and backing of the people affected.

4. Coaching and Building a Team to Achieve the Vision

Individual and team development are important activities carried out by transformational leaders. To develop a team, leaders must first understand team dynamics. Several well-established and popular models describe this, such as Belbin's Team Roles approach, and Bruce Tuckman's Forming, Storming, Norming, and Performing theory.

A leader will then ensure that team members have the necessary skills and abilities to do their job and achieve the vision. They do this by giving and receiving feedback regularly, and by training and coaching people to improve individual and team performance.

Leadership also includes looking for leadership potential in others. By developing leadership skills within your team, you create an environment where you can continue success in the long term. And that's a true measure of great leadership.

The words "leader" and "leadership" are often used incorrectly to describe people who are actually managing. These individuals may be highly skilled, good at their jobs, and valuable to their organizations – but that just makes them excellent managers, not leaders.

So, be careful how you use the terms, and don't assume that people with "leader" in their job titles, people who describe themselves as "leaders," or even groups called "leadership teams," are actually creating and delivering transformational change.

A particular danger in these situations is that people or organizations that are being managed by such an individual or group think they're being led; but they're not. There may actually be no leadership at all, with no one setting a vision and no one being inspired. This can cause serious problems in the long term.

Leadership can be hard to define and it means different things to different people.

In the transformational leadership model, leaders set direction and help themselves and others to do the right thing to move forward. To do this they create an inspiring vision, and then motivate and inspire others to reach that vision. They also manage delivery of the vision, either directly or indirectly, and build and coach their teams to make them ever stronger.

Have you already identified what type of leader you are? If not, perhaps now would be a great time to? Leadership is a skill we must all master if we are going to ensure we continue to travel OUR journey to OUR destination. And how about the times when your not able to lead the way, have you considered in whom you have sufficient trust to assist in the leadership of this epic journey, who else shares your vision who can assist so collectively we are still on course? It's certainly not about bullying or cohering, but rather inspiring the right people at the right time to help us on our way to our destination.

Perhaps it would be a great idea to determine exactly what type of manager / leader you are, and what the successful business you are going to build requires? If it needs something different to what you are right now, it's a great idea to determine WHO may be best to lead and how you as the owner can inspire them to 'take the helm' and lead you and your business to victory.

Being the owner doesn't deem you always have to lead from the front, after all Churchill is reported to have said "I may not be the brightest, but I'm wise enough to surround myself with those that are!"

OPENNESS & CONFLICT

Julies Caesar once proclaimed "My left is already dead, my right in retreat and the centre giving way; the situation is an excellent time to attack" With well-founded strategy, inspirational leadership and determined followers **anything** is possible. He, who sows doubt, is the first to fail, "The man who says I CAN, and the man who says I CAN'T will both be right" – Henry Ford

Never be afraid to FAIL, after all FEAR is merely an acronym for FAILURE, EXPECTED AND REALISED. Don't follow someone else's rules, no-one ever became successful for following someone else's system; CREATE your own future; its back to that first question of not WHAT do you want to be? but WHO do you want to be?

I want you to do me a favour, I want you to look yourself in the mirror and sack yourself. I want you to tell yourself, and believe it, YOUR FIRED!

However, before you break down in tears or reach for the scotch, I want you to know there's a position just become available, and according to the job specification I think you might be ideal. When you go to work tomorrow, I want you to consider yourself on probation, and that your being closely observed to determine if you are what the company is looking for. Its only if we continually consider this as a trial, our probation that we will not sink (regardless of how keen we are not to) into the mediocre realms of complacency, and spiral into that vicious circle of contentment. There are far too many people holding good jobs, great job, fabulous opportunities hostage, preventing them from the freedom to discover their own dreams and the right person for realizing theirs!

Now I want you to consider your relationship. Re-consider the 'job specification' for that honorary role, and determine if you're still living up to those requirements. I attended a friend's wedding recently, and was initially horrified to hear the vicar as part of the sermon advise the 'wife to be' to tell her husband of all her dreams, aspirations and desires, then lay them aside and spend her life assisting him in achieving his. My Equality button was on overload, and I was ready to stand and object to such advice.
Thankfully, the lessons I learnt from hours, days, weeks of waiting for something to happen on various operational tours enabled me to remain patient long enough to then hear the vicar then advise

the 'husband to be' exactly the same! Its only when we work collectively to achieve the greater goals in life than our personal attainment that we can truly live a life of worth, value and emotional attainment, and this is far more satisfying than any personal achievement at the sacrifice of all others.

I have previously worked in two very different culture environments even though they were predominantly providing the same type product/service. The first an exceptionally open, honest, all hands to the pump type of business where managers 'mucked in' and leaders led by example. Communication was open, flowing and very engaging. Anyone was willing and able to ask questions and debate the response; it was a healthy successful business with a great culture, people and prospects. The other was a business which offered the same products & services but was significantly bigger, it had many staff, many business locations, it was to the outside world the countries largest provider of these products & services, but quickly after joining there I found internal communication was poor, disjointed and only one way. Management maintained a 'do as I say not as I do' approach, with 'secret' meetings, closed door agenda's and a whole myriad of mixed messages from many different sources. The lack of open discussion, caused conflict, resentment, a complete 'them and us' culture which stifled growth and caused relentless un-necessary problems including a high sickness absence record and countless resignations from some exceptionally talented and capable people.

From over 12 years in the British Armed Forces, and a significant amount of time 'on the front line' I've seen more than my fair share of conflict. However, prevention is far better than cure; and understanding what causes conflict in the first place is instrumental in understanding how to manage and resolve this volatile subject

Strategies to avoid conflict

1. Don't be afraid of conflict. Too many of us become agitated when we encounter conflict or disagreement out of concern and fear. It's odd when you think about it because conflict is a part of nature, a part of life, and unless you are a hermit, odds are that it's inescapable. You need to approach conflict calmly, as an expected part of dealing with others. Consider conflict as a way of learning to see things in a more clear way.

2. Abandon the concept of winning and losing when faced with conflict. Instead, adopt a strategy of resolution. Unless you are on a battlefield, chances are the person you come into conflict with is not the enemy, but instead someone whose goals are generally the same as—or at least interrelated with—yours. So instead of approaching the

conflict with the attitude of stopping it, think of redirecting the energy toward a common target. War is part of our nature, but the most successful societies have been built on cooperation. And common goals are great unifiers. When the other side senses that you are interested in finding a solution—common or not, yet—you likely will have created an ally where a potential adversary once stood. Rather than confrontation, you can work together in collaboration to find a solution that suits both sides.

3. Avoid negative or confrontational language. Stop using "buts" and "you're wrongs." Try using positive language that disarms rather than confronts, like, "I can see your point, and here is where I'm coming from…" or "I understand your position, and…"

4. Talk through the situation with a neutral party to gain perspective and clarity from that person. It is always helpful to get a problem out in the open. People you trust and who understand your frame of reference can provide valuable input. They can help you better understand what you are going through and tell you, for better or worse, whether they think you have properly judged or handled the situation.

5. Find something to distract you from the conflict. Distance yourself from the problem. Start a new project, plan a family outing or take off on a vacation or weekend getaway. Sometimes you have to clear your mind. The time allows you to re-evaluate your position and maybe even come back with a fresh perspective of how to resolve that nagging conflict.

Visit **www.Battlefield2Boardroom.co.uk/conflict** to download our 360-degree feedback template to understand more about how to ensure openness and effective communication within the workplace to prevent any conflict from arising.

So stop sitting in that life of comfort and security, that's not living its merely existing. Start stretching those comfortable boundaries we have allowed ourselves to become sheltered by. They have shackled your inspiration, muted your drive and buried your determination. Remember in chapter one, we have already discovered life is an adventure, so set sail and re-discover.

MUTUAL COOPERATION

"If you wanna go fast go alone" Fast may be fun, but alone soon becomes boring *"If you wanna go far, go together"* Let me give you the most powerful bit of advice I can give: Before you take, give. There is NOTHING more rewarding than to give, nothing more satisfying than to see someone else happy, nothing more exhilarating than to make a stranger smile; try it sometime. No, try it today.

I've already recognized within this text, Lance Corporal Paul Scrace was my saviour, an unspoken, mutual cooperation. Who's yours? And more importantly who are you cooperating with right now, just like the vicar stated, who are you supporting to help realize their dreams, their goals, their objectives.

During my military career, I spent some time posted to Catterick Garrison, North Yorkshire. One day on leaving the corporals mess I heard the distinctive sound of a soldier being "doubled marched" to the guardroom after having been charged for breaking military law. The regimental policemen had the solider racing towards the guardroom at a rapid pace of knots whilst carrying his ironed military uniform ready to be inspected, it was a warm summers day and before long, the soldier having missed breakfast and rather dehydrated from his excessive exercise fainted. Immediately the Regimental Guard yelled "MEDIC" and 2 private soldiers from my section were seen running directly to where the soldier lay. From a distance I proudly watched as the first soldier went text book through all the correct drills of checking to ensure there was no dangers, no response from the unconscious man, that his Airway was open and clear and that he was Breathing, before smartly and professionally rolling him into the recovery position at the roadside.

However, my pride quickly turned to horror and disappointment as the second medic then went on to lift his legs leaving the side of the soldiers face pushed firmly into the road as his feet were now being held approx. 18" off the ground. I ran to the scene to correct the second soldier who had mistaken unconsciousness for 'feeling fait' whereby the correct drill is to lay the patient down and raise the legs to allow more oxygenated blood to return to the head and heart thus preventing a faint!

However, I didn't arrive at the scene prior to the Commanding Officers staff car being driven past, halting and the window lowering "What on earth are you doing?" (Questioned the Commanding Officer) The first soldier began to explain the soldier was unconscious and so was in the recovery position, but the Commanding Officer interrupted pointing at the second soldier "No, YOU. What an earth are YOU doing?" sheepishly, cautiously the second soldier replied "Protecting my best boots Sir!" Cooperation comes in many forms, (as this soldier had loaned his prize pair of highly polished parade boots to his now fallen colleague!

Esop's Fables teaches us 'One in the hand, is worth two in the bush'. I've often found it far better to give without compromise, without expectation than to have parameters or conditions.

Returning to the African proverb do you want to go fast or far? Fast is fine, but lonely and unsustainable, Far may be a little slower to start with, but a TEAM takes you places you would NEVER have achieved on your own, because Together Everyone Achieves More.

From the references to Jim Collins 'Good to Great' we have already mentioned, your already aware its all about not only being part of a winning team, buts about ensuring they aim to win at the same game as you! We have to have a game plan, that EVERYONE buys into, willing to give their all for, willing to give up any notion of individual successes in pursuit of team achievements. I remember reading once of an Olympic team rower who at every individual practice would not stop training until he passed out! Only to wake and start training again! When questioned about his extreme training habits he simply replied "I have to be prepared to do more than anyone else in that race. I owe it to my team"

From a military perspective, I also know first hand the incredible reliance on TEAM. From prior to you ever setting foot on a Military Barracks for the first time, you are designated a number, which for the first 12-16 weeks almost replaces your name and anything else of your own identity. For months, (in some circumstances, years) I was 866 Allen! Part of a team, a cog in a wheel. But it was because I was a cog that enabled me to grow the reliance, the understanding of the support & camaraderie that comes from being in a winning TEAM.

Throughout my military career, TEAMS surrounded me. Yes we were all part of the British Armed Forces, and my team wore Green (Navy Blue, Air Force Grey!) but there were so many teams within teams, from Regiment, company, platoon, section, through to football, rugby, cross country and boxing! The competitive spirit was very much alive and kicking and the reliance on each other to survive and thrive was paramount.

I've enjoyed a variety of roles and responsibilities since leaving the Army, including working for both large and small companies as well as self-employment & entrepreneur. I've learnt lots, embraced change, welcomed the challenge and succeeded within my goals and having reached the majority of my goals, but it wasn't until I stopped one night and really drilled down into why I still felt there was something fundamentally missing, something wrong, something I HAD to find and fix! It took me many attempts of soul searching, trying new and different things, getting involved in a whole range of different opportunities in search of this elusive missing ingredient, so illusive I had not yet found.

Then one day, and almost out of no-where it struck me, I was lonely! And although I worked with a great 'bunch a guys' and was having a whale of a time, I wasn't part of a team.

The bookings would come in, the work was getting done, invoiced were paid everything couldn't really have been much better, but something had been missing. Throughout all my career I'd been responsible for being a cog in a wheel, part of a team, I'd worked as part of something bigger than just me, and here I was, standing in front of hundreds if not thousands of people as a keynote speaker, inspiring them to do something different, trying something new, to stop what they had been doing, step out from their comfort zone and 'live a little' and all I wanted was to go back to being part of a team, my own security blanket of normality!

Teams are incredible vital components if we are truly to achieve all we wish to. You see, you can't be at 100% all of the time, and the more you try to be; the more unlikely you are to achieve 100% at all, but life, our mission, our goal and purpose demand 100% of us in order to succeed. Its only when we have a strong, positive team of people around us, be it family and friends or team mates and colleagues that we will continue to push ourselves harder, work smarter and become better than we would have otherwise been in order for the TEAM GOAL to be achieved.

We invariably compromise ourselves. We find excuses (legitimate or otherwise) as to why we haven't quite achieved EVERYTHING we were capable of. Exceptionally few will ever push themselves to the absolute limit every time they get the chance. But when your part of something bigger, your 'letting the team down' if you don't give it all, especially when you see they are giving it their all too as an equal part to the overall success of the task. So when the task is big enough, and the right people form a team to achieve ANYTHING becomes possible.

How to Be a Good Team Player - Maximizing Your Contribution

Have you worked for teams where everyone pitches in, and you all work together in perfect harmony? Do you always play to your strengths in a team, or are there times when the group you're in just doesn't gel?

Either way, team working is such a vital way of completing projects that it's worth developing and refining the skills that will help you make a valuable contribution to whichever type of team you're in.

Sports teams are perfect examples of how many players working together can achieve much more than one player who is acting alone. For example, you may not be the best goal scorer, but you're great at moving the ball forward. You know that if you pass that ball to the person who **can** score, the team has a better chance of winning. Everyone on the team plays a different role, according to their strengths – and by helping and encouraging one another along the way, you can make some inspiring things happen.

Off the sports pitch and back in the workplace, we hear the term "good team player" a lot. But what does this really mean in a business context? What do leaders want from their team members, and how can you make a more significant contribution to your team?

These are some of the questions we address in this article. We show you what makes a good team player, and we offer some tips on how to make a bigger contribution in the future.

The Importance of a Good Team Player

Teams are created for several reasons. They may need to deliver a one-time project, or work together on an on-going basis. Either way, if you take advantage of a group's collective energy and creativity, the team can accomplish much more in less time.

What does this mean for you? Well, teams are probably an integral part of how things are done in your organization. If you show that you have the ability to work well with others, this could have a major impact on your career.

Being a valuable team member can open new career opportunities, because leaders may see first hand what a great job you're doing. You may even be invited to bring your strengths into play in another team setting – and in higher profile, business-critical projects. This is why learning to be a good team player is so important. If you make a good impression, you never know what possibilities might open for you.

Use Your Strengths - Do you know what you do best?

Perhaps you're incredibly organized. Or, you might excel at motivating people, helping resolve disagreement, or researching hard-to-find information.

Whatever your strengths, you have something valuable to offer. Find a role within your team that allows you to do what you do well. This will help you make a meaningful contribution – and increase your chances of doing a great job. Plus, it's usually much easier, and more satisfying, to do tasks when you're naturally good at them.

Teams usually come together to handle an issue that's difficult, if not impossible, for people to do on their own. When a group works well together, creativity levels are generally higher, as people tap into one another's strengths. This often leads to increased productivity, and an inspiring sense of collaboration and cooperation that moves everyone – and the project – forward.

The most successful teams don't just combine different technical skills; they also allow members to take on more general roles that cross-traditional functional line. Here, we've outlined three different models, which show you what these roles are.

The Belbin model says that people tend to assume "team roles" – and there are nine such roles that underlie the team's success. These roles are as follows:

- Shapers – people who challenge the team to improve.
- Implementers – the people who get things done.
- Completer-Finishers – the people who see that projects are completed thoroughly.
- Coordinators – people who take on the traditional team leader role.
- Team Workers – people who are negotiators, and make sure the team is working together.
- Resource Investigators – people who work with external stakeholders to help the team meet its objectives.
- Plants – people who come up with new ideas and approaches.
- Monitor-Evaluators – people who analyse and evaluate ideas that other people come up with.
- Specialists – people with specialist knowledge that's needed to get the job done.

Team leaders use the Belbin model to make sure there is the right balance of strengths and weaknesses on their team. Visit www.Battlefield2Boardroom.co.uk/team to learn more about Benne & Sheats Group Roles & Margerison McCann's work on Team Management Profiling.

INDIVIDUAL DEVELOPMENT

We may have hosted the London 2012 Olympics & Para-Olympics, and more recently the commonwealth games in Scotland, and done extremely well in all; and began a legacy of promoting 'Sport for all' and it's all about taking part. However, on the battlefield and in business silver medal, or second place doesn't count. Being 'runner up' to the company that won that multi million pound contract does cut it, so a do or die mentality is often required.

In the Army, your face either fits, or it doesn't; you've ether got it, or you haven't. There is a level, a grade, a requirement to meet a standard at WHATEVER cost. Meet the grade and your in (and that's when the training REALLY starts) don't meet it and there's a question to be answered, was it because you were unable or unwilling? Unable and that could well be a training need, either physical or mental, unwilling and your soon shown the door, there's no room no for wannabe's and sponges!

Look around you and determine who's got it. Got what it takes to survive, who's got that edge that means when your feet are to the fire, when the pressure is on and you REALLY need to pull out all the stops and PERFORM, who will be with you, who will still be there encouraging you, supporting you, pushing you to continue achieving? Or, will they have left you alone? Are they the type that's off in one direction regardless of who's with them? There is also the scary reality that it could be them who have jetted off as a team into the sunset, and left only the stragglers behind! Its at this point you need to ensure your still in the leading group, and not stood with a small bunch of others asking the question "Where did everyone go!" If that's the case, you've just hit a stony reality its time to think about getting off this bus!

...So, your still here! In which case it's about further learning. As mentioned earlier, life's a journey of discovery, of change and challenge, as my Nan would say 'A day without learning something, is a day wasted' its ALL about the discovery.

You might consider reading this as part of your learning, your Continual Professional Development, however whilst reading is an hugely important (yet under utilized skill amongst many) it's the IMPLEMENTATION of that learning that will set us apart from many a Scholar who spends their time learning, without every applying that in a practical sense.

Throughout the last few chapters, we've looked at many ways in which you can spend time self-discovering your inner you. The goals, ambitions, dreams of yesteryear, and found ways in which you can break free of the norms of today to determine a different result for tomorrow. But it's only when you put this learning into action does anything actually occurring.

That life long adage "If you always do, what you've always done, you'll always have, what you've already got" has never been truer than right now. If you want something different, you have to do something different, you'll never get a different result from doing the same action time and time and time again.

For over 12 years my career was as a soldier. There was a set routine that I (and so many others followed) which collectively 'got the job done' and whilst there were many a time when the actions of the day were exceptionally unpredictable, the actions we carried out were not. We worked as a team, through a routine of pre-determined drills, with skills and precision we had worked on countless times before so we knew the expected outcome. However, one day; my career was over. The decision of a medical review board determined I was no longer a solider, no longer 'fit to serve' My time within this role had quickly changed from indefinite to definite, and within a few short months of the decision being made, I was no longer a soldier, no longer a number, not part of that winning team, It's then all back to survival and self-discovery.

I had no acknowledgement initially of how institutionalized I had become. Reliant on the abnormality of the conditions to which we lived and worked, everything changed, everything had to change; in order to survive you had to quickly adapt to your new civilian surroundings, which may seem absurd to anyone not having lived inside the wire, but for someone who had grown so used to the wire, the thought of it not being there was just weird!

Self-Mastery - Learning Personal Leadership

Learn how to master your actions, emotions and impulses.

"Courage, hard work, self-mastery, and intelligent effort are all essential to successful life."
Theodore Roosevelt, former US president.

What do you think when you hear the term "self-mastery"? You might picture someone like a martial arts master – calm, focused, and in control at all times. Or, maybe you imagine people who have their lives planned, and are in control of their own future.

Do you show these traits on a regular basis? Do you feel in control of your career and your goals? Or, like many people, do you feel that you should take more control of your actions and emotions?

In this article, we'll examine what self-mastery is – and we'll look at what you can do to develop it within yourself.

What is Self-Mastery?

When you have developed self-mastery, you have the ability to control yourself in all situations, and you move forward consciously and steadily towards your goals. You know your purpose, and you have the self-discipline needed to do things in a deliberate, focused, and honourable way.

Self-mastery also means mastering your emotions, impulses, and actions, and is vital if you want to achieve your goals in life.

Think about people you know who don't have any self-mastery. They're probably impulsive and rash. They might let their emotions control them, yelling at colleagues when they're angry, and then being overly polite to make up for this later. They're unpredictable and, as a result, people see them as untrustworthy.

When you demonstrate self-mastery at work, you prove to your colleagues that you have the inner strength and steadiness needed for effective leadership. So it's well worth the effort to invest time developing self-mastery. You'll likely become a happier, more balanced person – and you'll find that opportunities arise because of this.

Developing Self-Mastery

Self-mastery is a broad term that covers many aspects of your personal and professional life. Developing self-mastery can mean working on many of these areas. (If so, it may be best to focus on one or two areas at a time, so you don't become overwhelmed.)

Look at the following areas of your life to develop self-mastery:

1. **Goals**

Self-mastery starts with a vision of how you want your life to be.

Think about people you know who have incredible self-discipline. Chances are that they know exactly where they want to go in life, and this vision gives them the strength to get there.

This is why it's so important to start with a clear vision of your short-term and long-term objectives. Learn how to set personal goals, and get into the habit of moving towards these goals every day.

The clearer you are about what you want to achieve in life, the easier it is to move forwards calmly and confidently.

2. Attitudes and Emotion

Your attitude and emotions play a major role in self-mastery. Those who show strong self-mastery don't let their emotions control them – they control their own emotions.

Focus on something positive every day. Be grateful for things, even if these are just things like that fact that you do a job you enjoy, or that the weather is beautiful on your drive to work. Having gratitude and a positive outlook will set the tone for the rest of your day.

Resist the temptation to blame yourself when things go wrong. Self-sabotage is a quick and cruel way of stopping yourself from reaching your true potential. If you find that you're undermining yourself, consciously make yourself stop. Instead, think of something positive and encouraging.

You can also change negative thinking with cognitive restructuring. Write down the situation that is causing your negative thoughts. Next, write down the emotions you feel, and list the "automatic thoughts" you have while experiencing these emotions. Then, list the evidence that supports these negative thoughts, and the evidence that refutes them. Finally, list some fair, balanced, objective thoughts about the situation.

Being able to manage and control your emotions helps you build emotional intelligence. This is your awareness of others people's needs and emotions, and your knowledge of how your own emotions affect those around you. Those who have good self-mastery are always aware of others, and they work hard to make sure that their emotions don't negatively impact other people.

3. Willpower

Think about how many times you've set a goal and, for one reason or another, never followed it through because of lack of willpower or self-control. It's happened to all of us, and we probably felt ashamed or disappointed that we didn't achieve what we wanted.

Willpower is an essential part of self-mastery. It's what pushes you forward to take action, even if you're feeling scared or hesitant. Willpower is also what keeps you moving towards your goals in the weeks or months ahead.

To boost your willpower, make sure you have both rational and emotional motives for what you want to achieve. For example, if your goal is to stop surfing the web in work time, a rational motive could be that it's against company rules, while an emotional motive could be that other people will lose respect for you when they see that you are not working hard.

For many of us, willpower comes in short bursts and is often strongest when we first decide to make a change. So, use your initial burst of willpower to change your environment, so that it supports your efforts to reach your goal.

For instance, imagine that your goal is to improve your self-confidence at work. At the beginning, when your willpower is strong, you could focus on changing the environment in your workplace by making a list of everything that hurts your self-confidence. You could also create a plan for overcoming those obstacles, and post items and affirmations in your office that provide reminders about your goal.

After a week or so, you might find that your willpower is not as strong. But, because you changed your environment, you're better prepared to continue working towards your goal, because you have a foundation already in place.

4. **Focus**

Improving focus is also key to self-mastery. For instance, how much time do you waste during your work day? How much time do you spend on the Internet, talking casually with colleagues, or getting coffee? What could you accomplish if you fully used the hours available to you?

Start by working on your concentration. Focus on one task at a time, and slowly increase your level of focus.

At first you may find that you can't concentrate on a task for more than one hour at a time, before you get tired and distracted. Try to increase this to two hours by adding 15 minutes of focused work every day. This will allow you to strengthen your focus to two-hour stretches – and then even more, if that's what you need to get things done.

Achieving self-mastery takes time and hard work, but it's definitely worth the effort.

It's best to work on one or two areas at a time. Start by identifying your life and career goals. Then, focus on maintaining a positive attitude during the day. Also, try not to let negative emotions impact anyone else.

Other strategies, like building your willpower and strengthening your focus, will help ensure that you keep moving forward toward your goals – whilst further building self-mastery.

Visit www.Battlefield2Boardroom.co.uk/development for further details on personal development and templates you may wish to download.

INTER-GROUP RELATIONS

Whilst I've already mentioned the British Military are considered as one of the most professional fighting forces in the world, I'm not arrogant or naïve enough to believe its still the era of the British Empire and we got here on our own. Throughout the ages we have learnt which battles to lose in order to win the war, who to show allegiance to, and who to stay well away from. Who to negotiate with, who to owe favors to and more importantly when to cash those favors in! Since 4 April 1949 and the signature of the Washington treaty, and the soon to follow formation of NATO there has been a modern alliance and inter group agreement as to a common ground an international working practice, which already tested from time to time, has formed a common groundwork of acceptable and non acceptable practice.

Relationships, be it within families, communities, departments, businesses also need to find that happy medium that allows each other to exist and grow. As the Internet enables more and more international connectivity there is a growing requirement for international acceptance and acceptability of who we are, what we stand for and how we live our lives.

The days of the Iron curtain have disappeared. Every day lives, relationships, atrocities and acts of symbolism are played out on the news, social media and the internet has created an instantaneous opinion so strong that governments, countries have fallen and risen on the strength of public opinion, international agreement or condemnation of decisions, actions or lack of, which has determined our whole existence is forever under the work microscope of consideration – the ramification of our actions has never had to be quite so considered as it is today.

Within the Army, each Battalion, Regiment, Company, Squadron, Troop is made up on hundreds of soldiers, all with varying backgrounds and opinions, yet works collectively to a common goal or purpose. In order to ensure we are able to survive and prosper in this world of Likes, pokes and unsubscribe, it's never been more important to maintain our own opinion yet be more tolerant of others.

As a nation we are now considered the most multi cultural society in the world, yet recent political studies suggest almost 1/3 of British society is as racist now as it was 30 years ago (a rise of approx. 5-12% dependent on whether geographical specific or not, with the capital the only city sited as being more tolerant than it was 30 years ago) Last years enemy have become todays friend and tomorrow who knows, the battles fought on our streets and in neighbouring countries have obscured the boundaries of who and what and where and when. Battles are no longer fought in trenches but over the Internet and with computer style consoles. Drones are the new spies and wars are being fought every day in the military sense as well as over the Ethernet highways for data supremacy.

In a previous chapter we have already discussed TEAM, and the importance of having the RIGHT people ON YOUR BUS. However, just as this becomes the norm, we have to come to the conclusion that for every rotation of the wheel, we are all being exposed to new sights, sounds and experiences. We are ALL learning, trying to find OUR Goal, OUR Mission, OUR purpose. This sadly means that whilst the team who we worked so hard to determine was the right team, sitting in the right seats on the right bus, when our journey began; the learning's we have all experienced along the way, may have now determined that some of the people currently traveling with you have subsequently determined this is no longer heading in 'their' direction; likewise, there may be others that are currently traveling with others, who see your bus as heading in their 'right direction'.

The parting of ways has rarely been easy, especially when we have shared so much, grown together so much, learnt together and shared previous successes together. However, parting will undoubtedly remain a part of our journey, as this journey is ultimately our own, and no one will ever TRULY realize their own destination whilst continuing to follow someone else's dream! So, as parting must also be a part of our journey, the manner in which this is executed is one of the last chapters for this book. 'Parting is such sweet sorrow' Shakespeare wrote all those years ago "But never more painful if done badly, with regret and bad taste". We learn much of each other through our journey together, we share, which is the only true way to collectively reaching the goals, but this also identifies weakness and as human nature is, we can also harbour greed, resentment the ability and willingness to sacrifice friendship and team goals for the pursuit of personal fulfilment.

All relationships therefore need to be managed, to ensure they stay healthy, that the goals, ambitions and aspirations of all concerned remain the same, and when they differ, the opportunity of open honest and meaningful dialogue may follow to determine if now is the time to stop the bus and let one or two off to seek their own goals.

It may be that you establish there are others, outside your existing business with whom there is mutual benefit in working collectively. Recently, we are seeing more and more shared ownership projects, the reinstatement of co-operative style arrangements and joint ventures.

Entering into a joint venture is a major decision, so here we observe an overview of the main ways you can set up a joint venture, the advantages and disadvantages of doing so, how to assess if you are ready to commit and what to look for in a joint venture partner.

Types of joint venture

How you set up a joint venture depends on what you are trying to achieve.

One option is to agree to co-operate with another business in a limited and specific way. For example, a small business with an exciting new product might want to sell it through a larger company's distribution network. The two partners could agree a contract setting out the terms and conditions of how this would work.

Another option is to set up a separate joint venture business, possibly a new company, to handle a particular contract. A joint venture company like this can be a very flexible option.

The partners each own shares in the company and agree how it should be managed.

You could also form a business partnership or a limited liability partnership, or even completely merge your two businesses.

To help you decide what form of joint venture is best for you, you should consider whether you want to be involved in managing it. You should also think about what might happen if the venture goes wrong and how much risk you are prepared to accept.

You may want to take legal advice to help identify your best option. The way you set up your joint venture affects how you run it and how any profits are shared and taxed. It also affects your liability if the venture goes wrong.

You need a clear legal agreement setting out how the joint venture will work and how any income will be shared.

Joint venture benefits and risks

Businesses of any size can use joint ventures to strengthen long-term relationships or to collaborate on short-term projects.

A joint venture can help your business grow faster, increase productivity and generate greater profits.

A successful joint venture can offer:

- Access to new markets and distribution networks
- Increased capacity
- Sharing of risks and costs with a partner
- Access to greater resources, including specialised staff, technology and finance Joint ventures often enable growth without having to borrow funds or look for outside investors. You may be able to use your joint venture partner's customer database to market your product, or offer your partner's services and products to your existing customers. Joint venture partners also benefit from being able to join forces in purchasing, research and development.

A joint venture can also be very flexible. For example, a joint venture can have a limited life span and only cover part of what you do, thus limiting the commitment for both parties and the business' exposure.

The risks of joint ventures

Partnering with another business can be complex. It takes time and effort to build the right relationship. Problems are likely to arise if:

- The objectives of the venture are not totally clear and communicated to everyone involved
- The partners have different objectives for the joint venture

- There is an imbalance in levels of expertise, investment or assets brought into the venture by the different partners
- Different cultures and management styles result in poor integration and co-operation
- The partners don't provide sufficient leadership and support in the early stages

Are you ready for a joint venture?

It's important to review your business strategy before committing to a joint venture. This should help you define what you can realistically expect. You might decide that there are better ways to achieve your business aims.

You may also want to look at what other businesses are doing, particularly those that operate in similar markets. Seeing how they use joint ventures could help you choose the best approach for your business.

You can benefit from examining your own business. Be realistic about your strengths and weaknesses - consider performing a SWOT (strengths, weaknesses, opportunities and threats) analysis to discover whether the two businesses are a good fit.

You should take into account your employees' attitudes and bear in mind that people can feel threatened by a joint venture.

It can also be difficult to build effective working relationships if your partner has a different way of doing things.

Choosing the right joint venture partner

The ideal partner in a joint venture is one that has resources, skills and assets that complement your own.

A good starting place is to assess the suitability of existing customers and suppliers that you already have a long-term relationship with. You could also think about your competitors or other professional associates. You should consider:

- How well do they perform?
- What is their attitude to collaboration and do they share your level of commitment?
- Do you share the same business objectives?
- Can you trust them?
- Do their brand values complement yours?
- What kind of reputation do they have?
- If you opt to assess a new potential partner, you need to carry out some basic checks:
- Are they financially secure?
- Do they have any credit problems?
- Do they already have joint venture partnerships with other businesses?
- What kind of management team do they have in place?

- How are they performing in terms of production, marketing and workforce?
- What do their customers and suppliers say about their trustworthiness and reputation?

Before you consider signing up to a joint venture, it's important to protect your own interests. This should include drawing up legal documents to protect your own trade secrets and finding out whether your potential partner holds intellectual property rights agreements. Also, it's worth checking to see whether they have other agreements in place, either with their employees or consultants.

Create a joint venture agreement

When you decide to create a joint venture, you should set out the terms and conditions in a written agreement. This will help prevent any misunderstandings once the joint venture is up and running.

A written agreement should cover:

- The structure of the joint venture, e.g. whether it will be a separate business in its own right
- The objectives of the joint venture
- The financial contributions you will each make
- Whether you will transfer any assets or employees to the joint venture

- Ownership of intellectual property created by the joint venture
- Management and control, e.g. respective responsibilities and processes to be followed
- How liabilities, profits and losses are shared
- How any disputes between the partners will be resolved
- An exit strategy

You may also need other agreements, such as a confidentiality agreement to protect any commercial secrets you disclose.

Ending a joint venture

Your business, your partner's business and your markets all change over time. A joint venture may be able to adapt to the new circumstances, but sooner or later most partnering arrangements come to an end. If your joint venture was set up to handle a particular project, it will naturally come to an end when the project is finished.

Ending a joint venture is always easiest if you have addressed the key issues in advance. A contractual joint venture, such as a distribution agreement, can include termination conditions. For example, you might each be allowed to give three months' notice to end the agreement.

Alternatively, if you have set up a joint venture company, one option can be for one partner to buy the other out.

The original agreement should also set out what will happen when the joint venture comes to an end. For example:

- How shared intellectual property will be unbundled
- How confidential information will continue to be protected
- Who will be entitled to any future income arising from the joint venture's activities
- Who will be responsible for any continuing liabilities, e.g. debts and guarantees given to customers

Even with a well-planned agreement, there are still likely to be issues to resolve. Good planning and a positive approach to negotiation will help you arrange a friendly separation. This improves the chances that you can continue to trust each other and work together afterwards.

Are you already forging relationships with others who can help? Have you already got strategic partnerships or Joint Ventures in place? It's far easier to achieve when we are all working towards similar goals, working collectively to share both the risk and reward. Who else is heading in your direction, who else has visions / goals similar to yours, who else could you create a relationship with in order to travel at least some of your journey with? The beauty of the internet is that the 6 degrees of separation from anyone else in the world has never been easier, just a few clicks and were connected with the world, so switch on, log in and search, you'll be amazed what and who you will find, and collectively start working towards something special, something different, something wonderful.

REVIEW

So the very last of the principles is to stop and review. This is a forever turning wheel we are on, and as soon as you get full circle its about reviewing where you've got to, and amending process, system, people, attitude, resource, destination to ensure its fit to roll again!

360 review, is often difficult, challenging. It can cause difficulty and upset the direction of travel, but vital if as a team were going to work together to one primary goal for the benefit of all concerned. It's about looking objectively at every aspect of the last circle to determine what works and what doesn't. What needs to be improved and what needs to remain.

Its about continually challenging 'the norm' to determine is there a better, faster, more efficient way of doing this, and what are the side effects, benefits, fall out from changing the current status quo.

It can be just as difficult to self-review. We can often be either overly critical and self damning of our own short comings, or just as impractical overly praising of our own ability our own capability and misguided competence. However, with a clearly written and agreed goal, set of objectives, plan to follow we can more easily review the plan without attaching any form of emotion to the effectiveness or otherwise of any particular party in its execution. Careful, open and meticulous regular review of the plan will enable us as a team to determine if we are still on course, what actions must be made to ensure we remain on course, likewise what future actions must be prevented to ensure the success of the mission.

After each 'contact' (encounter with the enemy) each section of soldiers will quickly have a 'round up' of what's occurred, the current situation, and how it affects the mission. The most successful businesses are ones where there is a mission statement, but the flexibility for those responsible for the actual implementation of the works in order to achieve the goal to allow for 'variables'.

We then take our learning's from this encounter, and run the 'test & measure' sequence we previously covered, to determine likelihood of a repeat, and to consider actions for the future.

This ensures every time we meet a new hurdle, problem, difficulty we can apply prior learning to ensure we are smarter, quickly, more efficient in overcoming it to proceed with the mission. It's only once this learning is then communicated clearly to leaders and teams that collectively we improve, and can all benefit from the experience.

Your review is just as important to this process, so please; take a moment to visit www.Battlefield2Boardroom.co.uk/Review and leave your comments, thoughts, suggestions, and feedback on this experience.

So there you have it! 10 Military Strategies I learnt throughout my successful career within the British Armed Forces, I have been able to utilize to hugely benefit my career, my relationships and my lifestyle since leaving the services.

But really that's only the beginning, after all Rome wasn't built in a day, and just because you have been kind enough to donate a few hours of your valuable time reading this book, doesn't automatically mean life will suddenly be different, its never been about the 'talk the talk' its about the 'walk the walk' its about putting this book down and implementing what you have learnt from it.

I've really enjoyed sharing this part of my journey with you, but now its time for you to continue yours. My thanks for sharing part of your journey with me, now put the book down and return back to walking your walk away from the Mediocrity Minefield and towards your newly identified goals of super success.

Made in the USA
Charleston, SC
07 October 2015